Increase Your Vertical Jump - 20 Exercises

How to Increase Your Vertical Jump

By Devon Gaines

Table of Contents

Introduction

The Vertical Jump is defined as our ability to leap as high off the ground as we can from two feet. A popular misconception is that we are allowed to take a few steps before the leap but in order to properly test the 'Standing Vertical Jump' we must begin from a stand-still.

For sports such as track and field, basketball, volleyball, and football, the Vertical Jump is key for athletic performance. Along with other special tests, elite athletes have their jump height monitored regularly throughout the year and if they do not reach the target height for their sport, the training program will be adapted accordingly. A 40 inch jump is considered good for sports which rely on vertical power. 50 inches is seen less often but is excellent. In a testing facility, Vertical Jump can be measured with state-of-the-art equipment such as pressure platforms that clock your air time or lightening accurate laser beams.

For those of us who do not have access to scientific fitness centers, we can test our own Vertical Jump height. Stand as tall as possible side onto a wall. Mark your middle finger print with some ink that will mark the wall. Reach your inner arm as high as possible, with your palm facing the wall and mark the wall with your middle finger. Try 5 jumps and each time reach your middle finger as high as it will go. Use what is called a 'counterbalance' movement with your legs and arms. In other words, quickly bend your knees immediately prior to your jump. The arms should move behind the body on bending the knees and as you extend your legs to power up, the arms should be straight to drive forward and up. The counterbalance movement in the legs and arms are vital for maximizing your vertical distance. Measure the distance between the two marks on the wall after your best jump.

Once we have measured our Vertical Jump and we fall short of our sport's requirements, what training methods and exercises should we implement for the next cycle of conditioning? Usually the athlete will undergo a combination of resistance training strength exercises as well as plyometrics. Plyometrics are exercises whereby the jump is preceded by a countermovement. The countermovement is effective as it relies upon the *stretch-shortening cycle*; a process whereby the muscle stores elastic energy as it lengthens which is then released into kinetic energy as the athlete jumps. Let's look at how more height can be achieved.

Power = Work / Time

'Work' can be increased by applying more 'force'. Basically, vertical jump will increase if we can apply more force output in a shorter period of time; the faster we can be with force, the higher the jump. Strength exercises such as Powerlifts can enable an athlete to generate more maximal 'force' although we should be aware that normally these lifts occur at slow speed so in fact a power lifter can be a lot less powerful than athletes in other explosive sports. Two important types of strength necessary for the explosive jump include 'starting strength' and 'reactive strength'. We have a greater starting strength if we are able to switch on as many muscle fibers as possible at the start of a movement. Reactive strength relates to our ability to apply force when moving from an eccentric (muscle lengthening) action to a concentric (muscle shortening) action. The following exercises include useful warm-ups and drills that will enhance many different types of strength for that all important Vertical Jump.

Exercises

Warm-Up Jump

You should try this before performing your strength routine, speed exercises or plyometrics. It serves not only as a warm up but can result in a higher jump. The warm- up starts by you jumping into the air but by moving only at the ankle joint. Remember that whilst you are in the air, you should pull your toes towards your shins (dorsiflex the ankles) but ensure that your heels don't hit the ground on landing. This is quite a short and sharp movement. The idea is that you spend as little time on the ground as possible. The key is to keep your knees locked by activating your quadriceps and avoid flexing your hips too much; stay in a straight line. Warm-up jumps can be executed at different heights. Low jumps are performed as quickly as possible and you will jump only 2 inches off the floor. The objective of high jumps is to jump as high as possible. Try the following: Low jumps - 3 sets, 20 seconds for each set, 30 seconds rest between sets. High jumps - aim for the same as the low jumps.

Hip Flexor Stretch (Static)

As a general rule, it is not a great idea to perform static stretches before exercises such as the Vertical Jump or those needing maximum power output. Static stretching can activate sensory organs in the joint called Golgi Tendon Organs and this can result in an inhibitory reflex on just the muscle we want to contract. We don't want to switch off the muscles working as prime movers in the jump! There is an exception to this rule. When we jump into the air we execute a movement that is known as the triple extension, which is the extension through the hip, knee and ankle. The hip flexors cross the front of the hip joint therefore they are effectively stretched by the triple extension movement or to put it another way, in order to fully extend and raise our arms, it is beneficial if our hip flexors are flexible so our hips can extend through the required range of motion.

If you statically stretch the hip flexors, they will 'turn off' and will lengthen more easily during the triple extension. Now, if you are tight through your hip flexors, you should get into the habit of stretching them every day. It is not hard to tell if you are tight in either of your hip flexors. You can use a mirror for this exercise. Sit on the edge of a high bench, hold onto one knee and lie back over the bench. Try to flatten your lower back slightly to avoid over-arching the spine. Let the free leg drop. Does the knee drop lower than the top of the bench or is it tight; does it hang high? Compare the other side. Hold onto the other knee and let the free leg drop again.

Does the knee drop lower than the other side - does it feel looser?

The static stretch should be held for at least 30 seconds twice on each side. Start in a lunge position with your right knee on the ground and your left foot forward as far as you can. Keep your abdominals strong but lean back slightly and raise your right hand in the air and side-bend off to the left. Really try to work deeply into the muscle. Breathe normally and the trick is to relax and lengthen the muscle as you breathe out.

Box Squat with Variable Load

This exercise is pretty demanding on the nervous system and so you shouldn't use this exercise in your program more than once a week. The idea is that, after each set, you don't allow your nervous system to recover fully so the rest period is limited. You allow enough recovery just so that you can complete each set with the same power output; muscular endurance will also improve. The load is varied by the amount of tension on the bands attached to the bar. As you move into the squat, the band tension will increase so total load will be a product of bar load plus tension in the band. The band tension will be at its greatest at the top of the squat; it will have lowest tension at the bottom of the squat. This basically requires the squatter to exert more effort as they ascend the squat. In other words, the squatter needs to accelerate in order to work the load concentrically. The squat is performed by creating a shoulder width stance with the feet; the toes should be turned out slightly.

Push the hips back as you lower into the squat but keep the chest as high as possible. You should breathe in as you lower into the eccentric part of the movement and breathe out when you are nearly at the top of the squat. It can be beneficial to vary the speed or tempo of the eccentric (lowering) part of the movement. Exercise tempos can be split into 3 numbers *-*-*. The first number indicates the duration of the lowering portion of the exercise. The second refers to the 'pause'. The third number tells us how many seconds the upward or concentric action should last for. 'X' indicates move as fast as possible! Try these three different tempos. Tempo 1: 2-1-X, Tempo 2: 1-1-X, Tempo 3: X-1-X. An athlete should be experience with squatting and practiced well for before trying this exercise. Aim for 1 or 2 reps per set. You could try multiple sets, perhaps 10-15 sets. Allow 1 minute rest between sets.

Gluteal Hamstring Raise (floor)

The Glute-Ham raise strengthens the knee flexors, spinal extensors and hip extensors. You can perform this exercise solo from the floor with or without an anchor such as a barbell with plates over the top of the ankles. You can also ask a partner to hold your ankles so they do not lift off the floor. It is essential not to bend from the hip; don't allow the hips to flex too much during the lower (eccentric) part of the exercise. Knee flexion happens to be a very important component of the jump so this is a very effective exercise. To complete the exercise, start in kneeling and lock your ankle joint. Keep the gluteals fired up, keep the chest up and start slightly tilted forward. Lower your hips and the whole of the upper body down toward the ground softly, just enough to tap the ground. You may use your hands to push lightly onto the ground if you need help back up. The lowering part of the exercise is what you should focus on; use good pelvic control. Try 10 reps for each set. You should attempt at least 3 sets with 1 minute between each set.

Reverse Hyperextensions

The apparatus used for Reverse Hyperextensions is a genius design. There is no other exercise out there that conditions the gluteals, hamstrings and lower spinal erectors quite like this one. Your position on the hyperextension table has to be correct in order to allow the pelvis to move freely. The aim is to maintain a lumbar curvature so the erector spinae muscles stay 'statically' contracted and are then able to 'stabilize' your body during the movement. In order to complete the exercise, lie face down with your torso and waist on the bench and hold onto the handles.

Tuck your chin in as this helps to avoid neck strain. The feet should be dangling but not touching the floor and your legs should be straight. Raise the legs, whilst keeping them straight and squeeze your buttocks at the top. Remember that curvature in the spine as you lower the legs to the floor. You may place a sandbag or weighted ball between the feet. Aim for 10 reps and complete 3 sets.

Weighted Swissball Crunch

You cannot forget about your "core" muscles. The rectus abdominus is one of the muscles of the core that flexes our spine and makes up the pillar that connects upper body movement to lower body movement. Any exercise involving a sequence of total body movements will require a strong core. We must be careful, however to avoid 'over-flexing' the spine especially when the core is loaded in any way. According to back specialists, flexion of the spine can put huge amounts of pressure on our spinal discs that is unnecessary for conditioning; little flexion movement is need to accomplish the functional strength we need in the abdominal flexors.

The Weighted Swissball Crunch is a perfect exercise for establishing just the right amount of bend in the spine for the rectus abdominus to get a good workout. Plus, the commonly under-used and weak neck flexors will need to get involved. Lie face-up over a Swissball so your lumbar spine is supported by the apex of the curve in the ball. Anchor your feet and try to keep your knee and hip joint fixed. Position your hands by your head and allow the head to tilt back slightly.

Initially, tuck your chin in to activate your deep neck flexors. Then roll your upper back off the ball slowly without rounding your shoulders (the distance between your breastbone and pelvis should shorten). This is the important part: raise up until all the abdominal muscles are fully contracted but do not roll up beyond this point.

16

You'll find your chest will end up just a little above an imaginary horizontal line and you should feel a great deal of shaking in the abs! Roll back down the ball.

The Swissball is a great piece of kit because it will support your lower back. Try 3 sets of 10 reps. If you can achieve 10 reps easily, add weight in 5 pound increments. Hold the weight at the top of your chest. You may feel safer anchoring the feet under a bar or have a partner hold your feet but try to push the feet to the floor as you crunch!

Floor Leg Raises

The core, unknown to some, is more than just the abdominal muscles. The core is actually made up of the abdominals, lower back and hip muscles. In addition to the visible 'six-pack' muscles (we all would like define a little more), the obliques or 'lower abdominals' are essential for pelvic stability. They are responsible for lumbar flexion, flexion to the side and rotation. In addition they assist the deep transversus abdominis muscle by increasing 'intra-abdominal pressure'; they help to support the vertebral column when it is loaded just when you land after a jump or squat with a bar for instance.

In order to carry out 'Floor Leg Raises', lie on your back with your legs straight and raised in the air. If you have flexible hamstrings your feet will be directly above your hips! Place your hands palms towards the floor under the curve of your lower spine. Try to flatten your lower spine by adding pressure to your hand. Now, lower your legs, keeping them straight and do not let the lower spine arch off your hands. 'Tap' the ground softly with your heels and then raise your legs again back to the starting position. You can make this exercise more difficult by holding weight between your feet. Breathe in as you lower your legs and breathe out slowly as your legs nearly reach their vertical position. Work with 3 sets of 10 reps to start and then add load or increase the repetitions.

Kettlebell Swings

This exercise is a dynamic, total body movement and requires fluidity. Remember that a vertical jump utilizes both the lower and upper body. In the same way, a Kettlebell Swing effectively activates a powerful hip extension movement simultaneously with shoulder flexion. Grasp a kettlebell handle in front of you with both your hands so that your palms are facing you (overhand grip). As you squat down, allow the kettlebell to drop between your legs.

It is essential at this stage, that you keep your shoulder blades squeezed together; push your chest out and up. Keep your weight on your heels and look slightly higher than the horizon line. Once you have reached the deepest part of your squat, explode up by extending at the hips and at the same time flex your shoulders so the kettlebell moves above your head. Make sure your keep your arms straight. Try increasing the weight by 5lbs each set. Try 3 sets of 10 reps. To work on your hip flexibility, you can put a small box under each foot which will allow the kettlebell to drop deeper between the legs.

Deadlifts

Deadlifts are really quite self-explanatory - you lift a dead weight from the floor. They are known as compound lifts; a perfect combination of knee and hip extension in order to lift as much weight from the ground upwards as possible. The prime movers for this exercise are the quadriceps (knee extensors) and the gluteals (hip extensors). The forearm muscles used for grip and the lower spinal muscles have to contract isometrically so that you don't drop the bar and your lower back shouldn't round. There are a few variations of grip on the barbell; mixed, overhand and underhand. These grips involve the placement of the hands at shoulder width.

The 'snatch' grip requires more flexibility from the hips; inevitably there will be a stronger recruitment from the powerful gluteals, hamstrings and lower back. These posterior-chain muscles are essential for the vertical jump so incorporate Snatch Deadlifts in your routine. Start with 3 sets of 10 reps to improve flexibility and form. Then, up the weight and perform multiple sets of 3-5 reps to increase strength. How do we measure the width of the hands for a snatch grip? Grip width is pretty individual and is dependent on many physical factors.

The easiest way to calculate your grip width is to hold your arms out, perpendicular to the body. Measure the distance between your left and right elbow joint. This should be where the middle fingers grip the bar. The foot stance should be about shoulder width apart and the toes should be slightly turned out. Grasp the bar with an overhand snatch grip and line the bar up so it is level with the base of your toe joints. Sit deep with your chest up and your shoulder blades squeezed together.

Position your shoulders so they are just over the bar. Look straight ahead and arch your spine as much as possible. Execute the lift by breathing in, brace your abdominals and drive powerfully off your mid-foot. Extend from your hip just before driving from your quads until the hips and knees are straight. The bar should stay close to the body at all times. Lower the bar carefully in reverse.

Trapezius Bar Deadlifts

When you look around most gyms, you will spot quite a large, strangely shaped diamond bar with handles on the inside. The idea is that you are able to stand within the diamond. By visualizing this, you can see that as the body can remain more upright during the lift as the load is not lifted from the front of the body but rather from each side. As a result the lower back is less stressed. This method can help lifters rehabilitating from back injury, who are worried about putting so much undue pressure through the lumbar area.

If you load plates on each side of the Trap bar, you will find that your depth is compromised. This is easily resolved by standing on a box a few inches tall; you will be able to reach new depths. This exercise follows the same principles as the Snatch Deadlift except that the grip is held each side of the body and the palms face inwards. Keep the chest tall at all times. Start with 3 sets of 10 reps to improve form and then increase the load on the bar until you are lifting your maximum weight for 3 to 5 reps. 6 sets of 3 to 5 reps is a good place to progress to.

Multiple Repetition 'Pulsing' Squats

This exercise is excellent to slip into a program about a few weeks before we are due a Vertical Jump test. Pulsing Squats come way up the list; always perform them before other exercises in your workout. In order to pick the correct weight, calculate 90% of your 1 rep max for a squat. So, if you can squat 200lbs only once, your target weight for this exercise, would be 180lbs. The goal is to squat about a quarter of your normal full squat depth. Perform 50 of these as fast as possible.

There is a lot of action at the ankle during a set of 50 reps. Reps 1-10 should be performed by lifting up onto the balls of your feet; tackle reps 11-20 with the heels on the floor; back to lifting onto the toes for reps 21-30; heels for 31-40 then finish with 10 reps lifting powerfully onto the toes once more. It really helps to maintain the same speed and squat uninterrupted throughout the whole set. You can also use bands attached to the bar with this exercise to improve your upward acceleration. There is the added benefit that the bands prevent the bar from bobbing up and down on the back of the neck.

Bulgarian Split Squats

The Bulgarian Split Squats are really a variation of the Single Leg Squat. Stand on one leg with your knee slightly bent. Place the top of the foot of your back leg on a small step. Keep your chest forward and keep your hips square (facing forward). If your hips twist, this may indicate that the back leg is too far back or that those hip flexors are lacking in length - they need to be stretched! This exercise achieves just that.

Hold a weight in each hand and lower your bodyweight until your back knee almost touches the floor. Then, drive back up to the start position. The gluteals of the front leg needless to say, will be in pain and your inner quad (the Vastus Medialis Obliquus) will need to switch on in order to keep that knee in line. As you must perform a set of squats on each side, they are effective for correcting muscle imbalances (check for postural differences each side). Try 10 reps each side for 3 sets. This exercise is fantastic for strengthening the hip and knee stabilizers which are key for efficient transfer of elastic energy into potential energy for that Vertical Jump.

Power Clean

The athlete will develop 'power' as a result of training with this exercise as opposed to the slow tempo Squats, Rows and Deadlifts. Power Cleans are performed explosively and are supposed to carry over much more effectively to movement patterns observed in most sports. Each muscle fiber is supplied by a neuron to make up a 'motor unit'. The motor units involved with powerful, short-lived activity are the Type IIBs. These require a greater level of 'activation' or neural drive in order to switch on.

It is lifts such as the Power Clean or Power Snatch that need a greater neural drive to the muscle fiber. In order to perform a powerful Vertical Jump, it is a good idea to be able to switch on these Type IIB muscle fibers, so get working on the Power Clean. The Power Clean is a complex movement which requires the direction of a trained eye by your side in order to perform it correctly. The basics are to stand over the barbell with the balls of your feet in line with the bar, hip width apart. Squat down and grip the bar with an over-hand grip which is slightly wider than your shoulders. Your shoulders should be slightly over the bar with your back arched very tightly.

Your arms should be straight. You should pull the bar off the floor by extending your hips and knees (a trained coach would say extend from the knees first whilst maintaining flexed hips). As the bar meets just above the knee, allow it to contact the thighs and powerfully raise the shoulders up and back and jump up by extending the body. The bar stays close to the body as it moves up and your elbows will flex out to the sides. Catch the bar on the shoulders by rotating your elbows around the front of the bar (keep them high). Do not allow the knees to bend lower than 90 degrees on catching the bar. Stand up. In order to lower the bar, bend the knees slightly and uncurl the elbows allowing the bar to drop to the mid-thigh level.

Keep a tight lumbar curve on the descent. You may unload the bar by uncurling the elbows and allowing the bar to drop in front of you with the hands lightly touching the surface of the bar - that is if you are using rubber weight-plates and the floor is very resistance to damage! The 'Power Clean' is performed for a maximum of 3 or 4 reps. You may lift for multiple sets.

The Push Jerk

This exercise has a huge vertical component. It transfers well to the Vertical Jump. It is easy to assume that the push of the bar overhead comes from the shoulders but in fact the power is meant to originate from the lower body. The feet start in a shoulder width position. Collect the barbell from a rack in front of you and walk back a couple of steps. You should carry the barbell on the front of your shoulders, with the elbows raised as high as you can. Your thumb should rest over the top of the bar.

Partially bend your knees and brace your abdominals. Jump as high as you can in the air. When the bar has reached its highest position (the highest point of your jump), you will push the bar over your head. Bend your knees slightly as you land on your heels and keep the bar overhead for a second. Lower the bar and walk forward to the rack and rest the bar down. Try 3 reps between racking the bar each time. Aim for 4-6 sets of these. The exercise transfers power from the lower to the upper body; this is another great reason for practicing it for the Vertical Jump.

Medicine Ball Throw

This exercise uses the same muscle groups as a previous exercise we have mentioned, the Kettleball Swings. The difference in this situation however, is that we are able to release the load and not worry about controlling it; we can exert more effort into the movement and create more explosion. Hold a medicine ball out in front of you at arms' length with your elbows slightly bent. Then, bend forward and powerfully toss the ball backwards over your head either into an empty space or to a partner.

If tossing into an empty space, you may want a few medicine balls next to you as you will not get a rebound! This is once again, a total body exercise that transfers power from the lower to the upper body; it is highly beneficial for improving your Vertical Jump. What weight do you start with? Start with 15lbs. You have to be aware of your surroundings - you don't want to toss that ball all the way into the cardio section of the gym. The ball should travel about 10 yards. If it travels much further than this, use a heavier ball. Try 3 sets of 10 repeats.

The Box Jump

The initial part of this exercise is just like the Vertical Jump. When you jump up onto a box, your arms should be positioned in front of your hips. This is a safety precaution. The Box Jump is a frequently used exercise in lower body exercise programs for elite athletes. Your feet should be hip width apart and your arms lifted up with the elbows bent. Bend the knees slightly and then fully extend the hip, knee and ankle without flexing the shoulders. Land on the box.

Drop off the box backwards quickly and extend your arms behind you. If your hips drop low enough that tells you that you have descended with enough speed. This is a remarkably effective exercise with a limited number of weeks to maximize your Vertical Jump. Aim for 3-5 jumps. You may perform up to 10 sets. Add small amounts of height to the bench as you get more explosive.

Seated Box Jumps

Seated Box Jumps are very similar to the Box Jump except that the exercise focuses more on the upward portion of the movement (the concentric action of the extensors). Sit on a bench placed a yard back from a box. Your feet should be hip width and your knees should be in line with your feet. Lift the feet a little off the ground at slow speed, drive them down hard and then jump powerfully up onto the box in front of you. Step back down carefully and repeat. You can hold a medicine ball to add load to this exercise. Hold it by your waist; not too high or you may hit yourself in the face! Try 3-5 reps and up to 10 sets.

Depth Jumps

Depth Jumps involve a high degree of loading to the joints. They are executed by literally stepping off (as opposed to jumping off) a box and then on landing you immediately jump upwards as high as possible. The higher the box, the greater the loading to the joints as you land; you raise the box height as you improve. If you step off the box, on landing the eccentrically loaded muscles stretch more easily. You are then able to contract the muscles during the upward movement much more quickly and with more force.

Let the body drop to where feels natural and then jump - do not try to absorb the impact slowly. In other words, try to limit your ground contact time. This exercise is typical of what we call a 'plyometric' exercise; it is used to enhance the elastic-reactive component of strength. As a rule, the athlete should aim for 0.2 - 0.4 seconds ground contact time. The shorter your ground contact time (amortization period), the faster and higher the jump will be.

If the jumper does not maintain form like a spring or look mechanically sound then the intensity of the exercise is too high. Depending on how experienced you are, start with a 12 inch box. Each week increase the box by 3 inches in height. Use a hurdle in front of the starting box to jump over - this will train your ability to land correctly on the second jump, or place a high marker that you must reach for; odds are you will jump higher if you must reach for something.

Linear Depth Jump

In the Linear Depth Jump, you are jumping up onto a second box following a drop off the first box. You are not landing on the ground from a height. This means that the body will receive relatively less impact compared to other Depth Jump exercises. It is a good introductory exercise and also helps the athlete to engage the correct arm position. The height of the second box may be a challenge for the athlete so it is wise to have a good base in plyometric training before raising the bar too high so to speak.

Drop off a 12 inch box onto the ground in front. On falling, your arms should swing back in preparation for the next move. When you touch the ground your hips, knees and ankles should be flexed and the arms positioned behind you; you are ready to jump. Drive the arms forward and bound on top of the box in front of you. Step down carefully and repeat. Try 3 sets of 10. Take a good 2 minutes rest between sets. Remember you should be landing on the front two-thirds (balls) of your feet. If your heels hit the ground, the likelihood is that your first box is too high.

Vertical Jump

This sounds a bit strange and kind of obvious but in order to get good at something specific, it's good to practice that exact drill. Your nervous system will then be primed for action. No matter how flexible or powerful we are, the right components don't necessarily bind together to make us an excellent jumper - technique is everything! Follow some of these important teaching points: On take-off, make sure your eyes and head are focused on wherever they are trying to reach (look high, jump high).

When the arms follow through on take-off, they should finish up in line with your ears - over-reaching or lack of arm drive can send you off balance or reduce your Vertical Jump height. Mark a spot where you take-off and land. You think it would be easy not to do but often times the jumper will land in front or behind the starting position and this can affect height. Last but not least, get those gluteals firing! The power comes mainly from the hips so the jumper should focus on this area.

If you found this book helpful, please feel free to leave a review on Amazon.com.

You can also visit my site at:
ExpertBasketballDrills.com

Made in the USA
San Bernardino, CA
31 January 2019